Bald Eagle

Kaite Goldsworthy

LET'S READ
AV²
BY WEIGL™
ADDED VALUE • AUDIO VISUAL

Go to **www.av2books.com**, and enter this book's unique code.

BOOK CODE

E222574

AV² by Weigl brings you media enhanced books that support active learning.

AV² provides enriched content that supplements and complements this book. Weigl's AV² books strive to create inspired learning and engage young minds in a total learning experience.

Your AV² Media Enhanced books come alive with...

Audio
Listen to sections of the book read aloud.

Video
Watch informative video clips.

Embedded Weblinks
Gain additional information for research.

Try This!
Complete activities and hands-on experiments.

Key Words
Study vocabulary, and complete a matching word activity.

Quizzes
Test your knowledge.

Slide Show
View images and captions, and prepare a presentation.

... and much, much more!

Published by AV² by Weigl
350 5th Avenue, 59th Floor, New York, NY 10118
Website: www.av2books.com   www.weigl.com

 Library of Congress Control Number: 2012940126

ISBN 978-1-61913-077-7 (hard cover)
ISBN 978-1-61913-300-6 (soft cover)

Printed in the United States of America in North Mankato, Minnesota
1 2 3 4 5 6 7 8 9 0 16 15 14 13 12

052012
WEP050412

Editor: Aaron Carr   **Design:** Mandy Christiansen

Photo Credits
Every reasonable effort has been made to trace ownership and to obtain permission to reprint copyright material. The publishers would be pleased to have any errors or omissions brought to their attention so that they may be corrected in subsequent printings.

Weigl acknowledges Getty Images as the primary image supplier for this title.

CONTENTS

What is a Bald Eagle?

A bald eagle is a bird of prey. This means it hunts and eats other animals for food.

A National Symbol

The bald eagle is the national bird of the United States. It is known for its beauty and power.

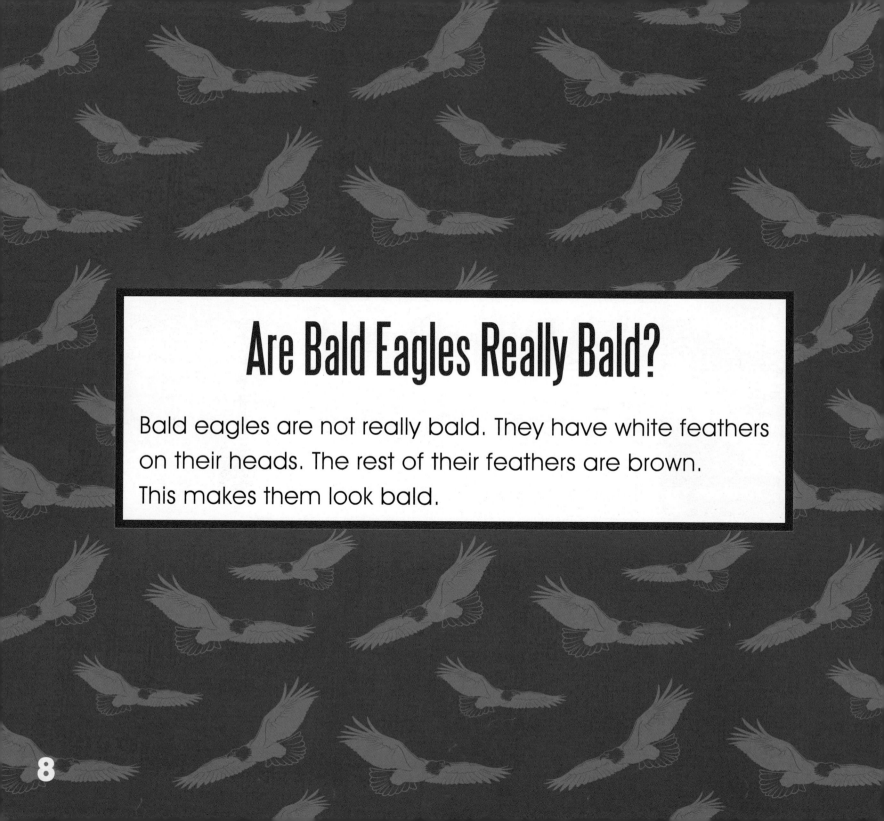

Are Bald Eagles Really Bald?

Bald eagles are not really bald. They have white feathers on their heads. The rest of their feathers are brown. This makes them look bald.

Where do Bald Eagles Live?

Bald eagles are only found in North America. They live near water and lakes. They build their nests high up on the tops of tall trees.

How Big are Bald Eagles?

Bald eagles are one of the largest birds in North America. The wings of a bald eagle can stretch up to 8 feet. That is longer than your bed.

What do Bald Eagles Eat?

Bald eagles like to eat fish. They catch fish with their claws. Eagles have very good eyesight. They can spot food from far away.

Becoming an Icon

A symbol is a shape or sign that stands for something else. Bald eagles are strong birds. They can soar high in the sky. A flying eagle often makes people think of freedom.

UNITED IN MEMORY
SEPTEMBER 11, 2001

18

The Bald Eagle on Money

The bald eagle is found on a very important U.S. symbol called the Great Seal. The bald eagle is also on some American coins and paper money.

Bald Eagles Today

Bald eagles are a protected species. This means there are special laws to keep them safe.

20

BALD EAGLE FACTS

These pages provide detailed information that expands on the interesting facts found in the book. These pages are intended to be used by adults as a learning support to help young readers round out their knowledge of each national symbol featured in the *American Icons* series.

Pages 4–5

What is a Bald Eagle? The bald eagle is related to other eagles, hawks, and vultures. Both male and female bald eagles are brown with yellow eyes, beaks, and legs, and a distinctive white head. They can live up to 35 years in the wild and almost 50 in captivity. Most bald eagles living in the wild never reach adulthood.

Pages 6–7

A National Symbol The bald eagle officially became the national bird and an emblem of the United States on June 20, 1782. The bald eagle is known for its loyalty. It is common for bald eagles to pair with a mate for life. Bald eagles are admired for their strength and beauty. The only real threat to the bald eagle's safety is humans.

Pages 8–9

Are Bald Eagles Really Bald? An eagle's head is actually covered in white feathers. This gives the bird the appearance of having a bald head. The bird's name comes from the old word "piebald" or "balde," which means *white*. Baby eagles, or eaglets, are born gray and do not develop white head feathers until they are four or five years old.

Pages 10–11

Where do Bald Eagles Live? Bald eagles are found only in North America. More than half of all bald eagles live in Alaska. They are often found near water. Bald eagles build their nests, called aeries, at the tops of tall trees or ledges. Eagles build the largest nests of any North American bird. Aeries can be more than 9 feet (2.7 meters) across and weigh more than 1 ton (0.9 tonnes).

Pages 12–13

How Big are Bald Eagles? A bald eagle's wingspan can range from 6 to 8 feet (1.8 to 2.4 m) long. Bald eagles can reach a height of about 3 feet (0.9 m). Most bald eagles weigh between 6 and 15 pounds (2.7 and 6.8 kilograms). Female bald eagles are larger and heavier than males.

Pages 14–15

What do Bald Eagles Eat? Fish are the main food source for bald eagles. Bald eagles are also scavengers. They eat between five and ten percent of their weight in food each day. Incredibly sharp eyesight allows them to spot prey from as far as 1 mile (1.6 kilometers) away. A bald eagle can swoop down to catch fish at more than 100 miles (161 km) per hour.

Pages 16–17

Becoming an Icon The United States chose the bald eagle as a symbol because it is seen as a majestic North American bird of great strength, courage, and longevity. The bald eagle also represents freedom, with its ability to soar through the skies and nest in high places. Bald eagles can soar to heights of more than 10,000 feet (3,048 m).

Pages 18–19

The Bald Eagle on Money In 1782, the bald eagle was chosen as a feature on the Great Seal to represent freedom and liberty. The bald eagle is found on many U.S. gold and silver coins, paper money, stamps, and other items. It is also featured on the president's flag and many state seals.

Pages 20–21

Bald Eagles Today Bald eagles were added to the Endangered Species List in 1978. Hunting, pollution, and pesticides caused their numbers to drop. Conservation efforts, as well as laws such as the Bald Eagle Protection Act, have helped stabilize the bald eagle population. Though they were removed from the endangered species list in 2007, bald eagles are still a protected species.

KEY WORDS

Research has shown that as much as 65 percent of all written material published in English is made up of 300 words. These 300 words cannot be taught using pictures or learned by sounding them out. They must be recognized by sight. This book contains 66 common sight words to help young readers improve their reading fluency and comprehension. This book also teaches young readers several important content words, such as nouns. These words are paired with pictures to aid in learning and improve understanding.

Page	Sight Words First Appearance	Page	Content Words First Appearance
4	a, and, animals, eats, food, for, is, it, means, of, other, this, what	4	bald eagle, bird, prey
7	its, the	7	beauty, power, symbol, United States
8	are, have, heads, look, makes, not, on, really, their, them, they, white	8	feathers
		11	lakes, nests, North America, tops
11	do, found, high, in, live, near, only, trees, up, water, where	12	bed, wings
12	big, can, feet, one, than, that, to, your	15	claws, eyesight, fish
15	away, far, from, good, like, very, with	16	freedom, icon, shape, sign, sky
16	an, often, or, people, something, think	19	coins, Great Seal, money
19	also, American, important, paper, some	20	laws, species
20	keep, there		

Check out www.av2books.com for activities, videos, audio clips, and more!

1 Go to www.av2books.com.

2 Enter book code. E222574

3 Fuel your imagination online!